ICELAND TR
GUIDE 2023

Your essential companion for planning an unforgettable trip to Iceland

Kathy R. White

Copyright © 2023 by Kathy R. White

All rights reserved. No part of this publication may be reproduced, distributed, or transmitted in any form or by any means, including photocopying, recording, or other electronic or mechanical methods, without the prior written permission of the publisher, except in the case of brief quotations embodied in critical reviews and certain other noncommercial uses permitted by copyright law.

TABLE OF CONTENTS

[My First Experience](#)

[Introduction to Iceland](#)
- [Location and Geography](#)
- [Climate and weather](#)
- [History and Culture](#)
- [Practical Information](#)

[Chapter 1](#)
- [Getting to Iceland](#)
- [By Air](#)
- [By Sea](#)
- [By Land](#)

[Chapter 2](#)
- [Planning Your Trip](#)
- [Best Time to Visit](#)
- [Length of Stay](#)
- [Types of Iceland visas](#)
- [Budget](#)
- [Accommodation Options](#)

Transportation in Iceland

What to Pack

Chapter 3

Top Attractions and Activities

The Golden Circle

The Ring Road

Blue Lagoon

Vatnajökull Glacier

Whale Watching

Hiking and Trekking

Icelandic Cuisine and Drinks

Chapter 4

Regions and Cities

Reykjavik and Surroundings

South Iceland

West Iceland

North Iceland

East Iceland

Chapter 5

Practical Tips for Traveling in Iceland
Money and Currency
Language
Safety and Emergencies
Etiquette and Customs
Health and Medical Services

Chapter 6

Conclusion and Final Recommendations

Top Do's and Don'ts
Off-The-Beaten-Path Destinations
Sustainable Tourism Practices
Conclusion

My First Experience

Iceland is a country that has been on my travel bucket list for years, and I finally got the chance to visit there last summer. As soon as I got off the aircraft, I was captivated by the distinctive scenery of the island. The air was fresh and pure, and the view was like nothing I had ever seen before.

One of the first things I did was hire a vehicle, since Iceland is a terrific destination to explore by road. The roads are well-maintained and simple to manage, and I found myself regularly pulling over to take in the beautiful vistas of the mountains, glaciers, and waterfalls that bordered the route. The Jökulsárlón glacial lagoon was among the sites I loved visiting the most. It was a tranquil spot, and the icebergs floating in the lagoon were stunningly gorgeous. I took a boat tour of the lagoon, which enabled me to get up and personal with the icebergs, and even spotted a few seals swimming about. Another highlight of my vacation was viewing the Blue Lagoon. The geothermal spa was wonderfully peaceful, and the warm water was the ideal way to unwind after a day of touring. I also got the chance to eat some of the local cuisine, including wonderful Icelandic lamb and fresh fish. One thing that struck me about Iceland was how simple it was to meet locals and other visitors.

The Icelandic people were really nice and hospitable, and I had some fantastic talks with residents and other visitors alike. Overall, my vacation to Iceland was a fantastic experience that I will never forget. The breathtaking natural beauty, pleasant people, and distinct culture make it a really remarkable visit. I'm excitedly looking forward to returning and exploring more of this amazing country.

Introduction to Iceland

In the North Atlantic Ocean, this country is situated. It's a Nordic island located between Greenland and Norway, and its nearest neighbor is Greenland. With a population of around 364,000 inhabitants, Iceland is the most sparsely inhabited nation in Europe. It is noted for its beautiful scenery, including glaciers, hot springs, geysers, lava fields, and waterfalls. Its unusual position also makes it a perfect destination for watching the Northern Lights, a natural phenomenon that draws travelers from all over the globe.

Iceland is a nation with a rich history and culture, stretching back to the Viking Age. The Icelandic sagas, a collection of medieval literature, give insights into the country's early history and are regarded an essential element of Iceland's cultural legacy. Today, Iceland has a sophisticated and vibrant culture, with a booming arts and music scene, world-renowned food, and a strong heritage of storytelling.

The Icelandic economy is mainly based on fishing and tourism, but the nation is also noted for its innovation in renewable energy, with geothermal power supplying the bulk of the country's electricity and heating. Iceland is also a pioneer in environmental conservation and sustainable development, with a strong emphasis on protecting its natural beauty and resources for future generations.

Overall, Iceland is a unique and intriguing nation that provides tourists a chance to explore spectacular natural landscapes, experience a lively culture, and see creative approaches to sustainability and conservation.

Location and Geography

Iceland's position near the Arctic Circle means that it has long summer days with over 24 hours of daylight, and long winter nights with very little daylight.

Geographically, Iceland is recognized for its rough and varied scenery. It is a volcanic island with more than 30 active volcanic systems, including the famed Eyjafjallajökull volcano that erupted in 2010, causing severe disruption to air transport. Iceland also contains multiple glaciers, with Vatnajökull being the biggest in Europe, occupying over 8% of the country's geographical area.

The nation is also recognized for its hot springs and geothermal activity, with the Blue Lagoon being one of the most popular tourist attractions. Iceland features several geysers and hot springs, which are utilized to produce power and provide heat for houses and businesses.

In terms of size, Iceland occupies an area of 103,000 square kilometers (40,000 square miles), making it the 108th biggest nation in the world. It has a population of roughly 364,000 people, with most of the population residing in the capital city of Reykjavik and the surrounding environs.

Iceland is separated into eight areas, each with its distinctive traits and attractions. The capital area, which contains Reykjavik, is the most populous and provides a variety of cultural and recreational activities. The southwestern area is home to the Golden Circle, a popular tourist circuit that contains some of Iceland's most renowned natural monuments, including Geysir and Gullfoss waterfall.

The western area is famed for its rough coastline, magnificent fjords, and wildlife, including puffins and seals. The northern area is noted for its spectacular vistas and outdoor activities like skiing and hiking. The eastern section is home to Europe's biggest forest, Vatnajökull National Park, and the spectacular Vatnajökull Glacier.

Iceland's location and topography contribute to its distinctive and diversified scenery, which draws people from all over the globe. From its active volcanoes and glaciers to its hot springs and geysers, Iceland offers a plethora of natural marvels to discover and enjoy.

Climate and weather

Iceland's climate is heavily impacted by the surrounding ocean currents and the polar jet stream. It is typically classed as subarctic, characterized by lengthy, cold winters and pleasant summers. However, the weather in Iceland is noted for its unpredictability and quick shifts, with high winds, heavy precipitation, and numerous storms throughout the year.

Winters in Iceland, which extend from November to March, are marked by long nights and short days. The average temperature during this period varies from -1°C to 4°C (30°F to 39°F), with the coldest months being December and January. Snowfall is frequent, especially in the northern and eastern areas of the nation, and may often linger for many months. Strong winds and blizzards are also prevalent throughout the winter months, especially in the mountainous areas.

Spring in Iceland begins in April and lasts until May. During this season, the snow and ice begin to melt, and the days gradually start to become longer. However, spring weather may be erratic, with heavy showers and windstorms. The temperature at this period varies from 2°C to 8°C (35°F to 46°F).

Summer in Iceland is brief, lasting from June through August. The temperature during this period fluctuates from 10°C to 15°C (50°F to 59°F), with rare heatwaves pushing temperatures beyond 20°C (68°F). Despite the comparatively moderate temperatures, summer weather in Iceland can still be unpredictable, with regular showers and windstorms. The extended hours of sunshine, with the sun frequently sinking as late as midnight, making summer a wonderful season for outdoor activities, like hiking, camping, and fishing.

Autumn in Iceland begins in September and lasts through October. During this season, the days begin to become shorter, and the temperature progressively declines. The average temperature at this period varies from 5°C to 10°C (41°F to 50°F).

Like spring, fall weather in Iceland may be unpredictable, with heavy rain and windstorms.

In addition to its periodic weather patterns, Iceland is also recognized for its severe weather occurrences, including blizzards, storms, and floods. The country's placement on the Mid-Atlantic Ridge, a geological border between the North American and Eurasian plates, also renders it prone to earthquakes and volcanic eruptions.

Note that, the climate and weather of Iceland are defined by long, cold winters, pleasant summers, and frequent rain and windstorms throughout the year. While the weather might be unpredictable, it is an integral aspect of Iceland's distinctive natural environment, making it a popular destination for vacationers and outdoor lovers.

History and Culture

History

According to the Icelandic Sagas, the first permanent settler of Iceland was Ingólfur Arnarson, who came in 874 AD. However, new archaeological evidence reveals that there may have been earlier occupations by Irish monks.

During the following several centuries, Iceland was controlled by chieftains who were constantly in battle with one another. In 1262, Iceland became part of Norway's dominion, and subsequently, in 1380, it became part of the Danish empire. Iceland achieved limited sovereignty in the 19th century, and in 1944, it became an independent republic.

Culture

Iceland has a distinct culture that has been formed by its terrain, history, and isolation. Here are some of the important features of Icelandic culture:

Literature: Iceland has a strong literary past, with the sagas being possibly the best-known example. The sagas are a collection of tales concerning the early immigrants of Iceland and their successors. Iceland has also produced numerous prominent writers, notably Halldór Laxness, who received the Nobel Prize in Literature in 1955.

Music: Iceland has a strong music culture, with several artists attaining worldwide renown. Perhaps the best-known Icelandic artist is Björk, who has received multiple honors and has been hailed for her distinctive style.

Language: Icelandic is a Germanic language that is closely connected to Old Norse. It has changed relatively little throughout the years, and Icelanders are proud of their language and their ability to retain their culture.

Art: Iceland has a strong arts sector, with numerous artists working in a range of mediums. One of the most prominent Icelandic painters is Ólafur Elíasson, who is recognized for his works that typically include natural elements.

Food: Icelandic cuisine is centered on the country's natural resources, including fish, lamb, and dairy products. Some classic Icelandic foods include hákarl (fermented shark), svið (sheep's head), and plokkfiskur (fish and potato stew).

Nature: Iceland's rough terrain is one of its most distinguishing qualities, and many Icelanders feel a close connection to the natural world. The country's geothermal activity has also contributed to the formation of several hot springs and geysers, which are famous tourist attractions. Overall, Iceland has a rich and distinctive culture that has been molded by its history and environment. Despite its modest size and seclusion, it has made significant contributions to the world in the realms of literature, music, and art.

Practical Information

Here are some useful facts for a visitor visiting Iceland:

Visa and Passport: Iceland is a member of the Schengen Agreement, thus if you are from a country that needs a visa to enter the Schengen zone, you will need a Schengen visa to visit Iceland. Make sure your passport is valid for at least six months beyond your scheduled travel date.

Currency: Iceland utilizes the Icelandic Krona (ISK) as its currency. While credit cards are frequently accepted in Iceland, it is a good idea to bring some cash with you, particularly if you are visiting remote regions.

Weather: Iceland is notorious for its variable weather, and it may change suddenly. Make sure you carry layers, waterproof clothes, and sturdy shoes.

Transportation: Renting a vehicle is the best method to see Iceland. However, public transit is also accessible in certain regions. Taxis are pricey, therefore it's preferable to utilize them only when required.

Safety: Iceland is generally a safe nation to visit, but it's always a good idea to take measures, such as avoiding leaving your valuables unattended in public places, particularly in popular regions.

Language: Icelandic is the official language of Iceland, however, most people speak English well, particularly in tourist regions.

Food and Drink: Icelandic food is distinctive, featuring delicacies such as pickled shark and Icelandic lamb. Alcohol is costly in Iceland, and it's exclusively available at state-run liquor shops called Vinbudin.

Tipping: Tipping is not common in Iceland, since service costs are frequently included in the bill. However, it's always appreciated if you get outstanding service.

Wi-Fi: Wi-Fi is generally accessible throughout Iceland, even in isolated regions. Most cafés, hotels, and restaurants provide free Wi-Fi.

Electricity: Iceland utilizes Type F sockets, which are the same as those used throughout much of Europe. Make sure you bring an adaptor if your gadgets have a different plug.

Chapter 1

Getting to Iceland

Getting to Iceland is quite straightforward, with various transit choices available, including plane and water travel. Here is some thorough information on the numerous methods by which you may go to Iceland.

By Air

Traveling by flight to Iceland is the most convenient method to access the nation for tourists arriving from overseas. Iceland is an island country situated in the North Atlantic, and there are two main international airports in the country: Keflavik International Airport (KEF) and Reykjavik Airport (RKV). Keflavik International Airport is the largest airport in Iceland and serves as the major international gateway to the country.

Here are some thorough facts about going by flight to Iceland:

Booking your travel: You may book your ticket to Iceland using any major airline, such as Icelandair, Delta, or United. Various inexpensive airlines operate flights to Iceland, such as WOW Air and EasyJet. You may book your flight online or via a travel agency.

Choosing your airport: As indicated before, there are two main airports in Iceland. Keflavik International Airport is situated around 50 kilometers southwest of Reykjavik, whereas Reykjavik Airport is located in the city core. Most international flights arrive at Keflavik International Airport, therefore it's advisable to use this airport if you're traveling to Iceland from overseas.

Admission criteria: Before coming to Iceland, you'll need to verify the admission requirements for your country. As of 2021, passengers from most countries needed to show a negative COVID-19 test result before visiting Iceland. You can see the newest entrance criteria on the official website of the Icelandic government.

Getting to your hotel: Once you arrive at Keflavik International Airport, you may take a shuttle bus or a cab to your accommodation in Reykjavik. The trip takes roughly 45 minutes by bus and 30 minutes via cab. Alternatively, you may hire a vehicle at the airport and drive to your hotel. If you're arriving at Reykjavik Airport, you may simply walk or take a cab to your hotel in the city center.

Transportation inside Iceland: If you're going to tour Iceland during your vacation, you'll need to pick a means of transportation. The most common alternatives include hiring a vehicle or riding a tour bus. There are various automobile rental businesses in Iceland, and it's suggested to reserve your car in advance. Tour buses are also a popular choice, and various firms provide guided trips to renowned tourist spots in Iceland.

Climate: Iceland has a subarctic climate, which implies that it's quite chilly throughout the year. The average temperature in Reykjavik varies from -1 °C in January to 11 °C in July. It's crucial to bring warm clothing, particularly if you're going to Iceland during the winter months.

By Sea

Traveling by sea to Iceland can be an adventurous and exciting way to explore the beautiful landscapes and unique culture of this Nordic island nation. Here are some important things to keep in mind if you're considering a sea journey to Iceland:

Routes: Iceland is located in the North Atlantic Ocean, and there are several routes that you can take to reach the island by sea. The most popular routes are from the UK, Norway, Denmark, and Greenland. You can find many different cruise lines and ferry companies that offer routes to Iceland, with different departure points and travel durations.

Time of year: The best time to travel to Iceland by sea is during the summer months, from May to September. This is when the weather is milder, and the sea conditions are generally calmer. It's also the time when there are more ferry and cruise options available.

Travel time: Depending on the route you choose, travel time to Iceland can vary from a few hours to several days. Ferries from the UK and Denmark can take up to three days, while cruises from Norway and Greenland can take up to a week.

Accommodation: Most sea journeys to Iceland include accommodation options onboard, including cabins with private bathrooms and shared facilities like restaurants, bars, and lounges. If you're traveling on a budget, there are also options for shared cabins and camping on some ferries.

What to pack: If you're traveling by sea, it's important to pack appropriately for the journey. This means bringing warm clothing, rain gear, and comfortable shoes for walking around the ship. You may also want to bring seasickness medication and other essentials like sunscreen and a hat.

Activities: While onboard, there are usually a variety of activities and entertainment options available, such as live music, movies, and games.

Some cruise lines also offer guided tours and excursions to explore Iceland's natural beauty and cultural sites.

Immigration and customs: As with any international travel, it's important to make sure you have all the necessary documentation and visas to enter Iceland. You'll need a valid passport, and depending on your country of origin, a visa or travel authorization may also be required.

By Land

Traveling to Iceland by land is an experience that many tourists dream about. Here are some things you need to know before you go on your journey:

Crossing Borders: If you are going by land to Iceland, you must cross the border from a nearby nation through a ferry. The two major ferry companies operating between Iceland and Europe are Smyril Line and Norraena.

Ferry Routes: Smyril Line travels from Hirtshals, Denmark to Seydisfjordur in the east of Iceland, with a layover in the Faroe Islands. Norræna runs from Hirtshals to Seydisfjordur through the Faroe Islands and from Hanstholm, Denmark to Seydisfjordur via the Faroe Islands.

Boat Schedule: Ferry timetables vary based on the season and the boat provider. It is essential to check the timetables in advance and purchase your tickets early, particularly during the peak travel season.

Documents: You will need a valid passport to visit Iceland, and in certain situations, you may require a visa, depending on your place of origin. It is advised to check with the Icelandic embassy or consulate in your country for the latest information.

Driving: Iceland is best experienced by automobiles, and there are several car rental companies available. However, it is vital to realize that driving conditions in Iceland may be hard owing to the weather and road conditions. It is essential to hire a 4x4 car and to verify road conditions before going on your trip.

Lodging: Iceland provides a broad choice of lodging alternatives, including hotels, guesthouses, hostels, and campsites. However, it is suggested to reserve your accommodation in advance, particularly during the high tourist season.

Weather: Iceland has a subarctic climate, which means that temperatures may fluctuate substantially depending on the season. It is crucial to bring warm and waterproof gear, especially during the hot months.

Currency: Iceland's currency is the Icelandic króna (ISK). It is preferable to convert your money before arriving in Iceland or withdraw Icelandic króna from an ATM.

Language: Icelandic is the official language of Iceland, however, English is commonly spoken.

Safety: Iceland is a safe nation to visit, however, it is necessary to be mindful of the weather conditions and to obey any safety standards or cautions. It is equally crucial to respect the natural environment and to leave no mark while experiencing Iceland's natural treasures.

Chapter 2

Planning Your Trip

Planning a visit to Iceland can be a thrilling and fulfilling endeavor. To optimize your trip, it's crucial to plan and take into account variables such as climate, transportation, lodging, and things to do. Iceland has something to offer everyone, whether you're a lover of nature, an adventurer, or a cultural enthusiast.

Best Time to Visit

When planning a vacation to Iceland, one of the most crucial elements to consider is the optimum time to visit. Iceland offers a variety of weather conditions that may fluctuate considerably throughout the year, and this might affect the traveler's experience.

The greatest time to visit Iceland is during the summer months, which occur between June and August. This season gives the longest prolonged daylight hours, with the sun never entirely sinking, offering tourists up to 24 hours of daylight. The average temperature throughout the summer varies from 10 to 15 degrees Celsius, with rare increases up to 20 degrees Celsius. This weather condition gives it an ideal opportunity to enjoy the country's natural beauties, such as glaciers, waterfalls, and hiking routes. The highlands, which are generally inaccessible during the winter months, are also accessible throughout the summer, making it a perfect season for trekkers and hikers.

Another motivation to visit Iceland during the summer months is the range of festivals and events that occur during this season. Reykjavik, the capital city of Iceland, offers a multitude of cultural and musical events, including the Reykjavik Arts Festival and the Iceland Airwaves Festival. The Viking Festival, which takes place in Hafnarfjörður, commemorates the country's Viking past with historical re-enactments and exhibitions.

For those who prefer a calmer period, Iceland's shoulder seasons provide a wonderful option. These months, which occur between April and May and September and October, provide a cooler environment and fewer people than the busy summer season. During the shoulder seasons, travelers may still experience spectacular natural scenery, such as the Northern Lights, without the invasion of people. The shoulder season is also a good time for whale watching since the waters around Iceland are home to a variety of whales and dolphins.

Winter in Iceland is another stunning and distinctive season to visit, with its snow-covered landscapes and ice-blue glaciers. The winter season, which comes between November and February, offers tourists a chance to view the Northern Lights, one of the most magnificent natural occurrences in the world. Winter sports, such as ice caving and snowmobiling, are also popular in Iceland this season. However, the winter season also comes with more extreme weather conditions, including snowstorms and blizzards, which may make it impossible to reach some of the country's attractions.

In essence, the ideal time to visit Iceland depends on the visitor's tastes and the sort of experience they wish to enjoy. For those wishing to enjoy the extended daylight hours and attend cultural events, the summer season is great. The shoulder seasons provide a calmer and warmer temperature, while the winter season delivers a unique and magnificent experience, albeit with more severe weather conditions. Whichever season you select, Iceland's natural beauty and cultural attractions are likely to make a lasting impact.

Length of Stay

The period of stay for a tourist in Iceland varies depending on the passenger's nationality and purpose of visit. If you are a citizen of a nation that is a part of the Schengen Agreement, you may remain in Iceland for up to 90 days during the 180 days without a visa. This applies to tourists, business travelers, and other non-EU nationals. If you are not a citizen of a Schengen Agreement nation, you will require a visa to visit Iceland, and the length of your stay will depend on the kind of visa you have been given. It's essential to remember that these laws and regulations may change over time, so it's always a good idea to check with the Icelandic embassy or consulate in your home country or the Icelandic Directorate of Immigration for the latest information.

Types of Iceland visas

The Iceland visa type you need to apply for is highly significant. The visa type outlines the papers you should provide and the activities you are authorized to do while in Iceland.

To pick what visa type suits you best, consider the reason why you desire to visit Iceland and what you intend to accomplish there. There are various kinds of visas to Iceland, based on your purpose of admission and term of stay. These visas are characterized as follows:

Iceland Transit Visa if you need to arrive in Iceland simply to take another aircraft or vessel to your non-Schengen destination country.

- Iceland Tourist and Visitor Visa if you need to go to Iceland for a short-stay journey of up to 90 days, during a six-month period. It is a short-stay visa for Iceland, and it enables you to travel across the complete Schengen region.
- The Iceland Business Visa is intended for individuals who are visiting Iceland for business purposes such as attending conferences or meetings, and who do not plan on staying in the country for more than 90 days.
- Iceland Cultural, Sports, and Religious Event Visa
- Iceland Medical Treatment Visa
- Iceland Long-Stay Visa

- Iceland Digital Nomad Visa

Budget

The cost of a trip to Iceland can vary greatly depending on different factors, including the length of stay, the season, planned activities, and personal preferences. Generally, a budget traveler can expect to spend an average of 90-120 USD per day, while a mid-range traveler can expect to spend around 200-250 USD per day, and luxury travelers can spend upwards of 400 USD per day.

When budgeting for a trip to Iceland, it's essential to consider various expenses, including accommodation, food, transportation, and activities. Hostels and guesthouses are the most affordable options for lodging, ranging from 30-70

USD per night, while hotels and Airbnb can cost more. Eating out in Iceland is pricey, with a typical restaurant meal costing around 25-30 USD. Budget travelers can save money by buying groceries and cooking their meals.

Since public transportation in Iceland is limited, renting a car is often necessary, starting at around 50 USD per day, but gas can be expensive. Iceland offers numerous outdoor activities such as hiking, glacier tours, and hot springs, but they can be costly, with some tours costing several hundred dollars.

It's important to note that peak travel seasons (June-August and December-January) in Iceland can result in higher prices, so it's wise to budget accordingly. Iceland also has a 24.5% value-added tax (VAT) on most goods and services, which can add up to the expenses.

Accommodation Options

There are numerous accommodation options available to suit your needs. These include;

Hotels: Iceland has a variety of hotels, ranging from budget-friendly options to luxurious accommodations. Icelandair Hotels, Fosshotels, and Kea Hotels are some of the most well-known hotel chains in the country.

Guesthouses: If you're looking for an affordable option, guesthouses are a great choice. Although they offer basic amenities such as shared bathrooms and kitchens, they provide an authentic Icelandic experience.

Hostels: Travelers on a budget, especially those traveling solo or looking to meet other travelers, can consider hostels. There are several hostels in Reykjavik and other towns and cities throughout Iceland.

Airbnb: Airbnb is a popular option for those seeking unique and personalized accommodations. You can choose from a variety of options, such as private rooms, apartments, or even entire houses.

Camping: Iceland's natural landscapes are breathtaking, and camping is a great way to immerse yourself in them. There are various campsites across the country, with varying levels of amenities.

Farmstays: For a distinctive experience, you might consider staying on a farm in Iceland. Many farms offer accommodations, ranging from basic guesthouses to luxurious options.

Glamping: Glamping, or glamorous camping, is gaining popularity in Iceland. Several companies provide luxury camping experiences, complete with comfortable beds, hot tubs, and private bathrooms.

Transportation in Iceland

As a traveler in Iceland, you have several transportation options available to explore the country. Listed below are some of the most popular ways to get around Iceland:

Car Rental: Renting a car is one of the most popular ways to explore Iceland. Many car rental companies are available at the Keflavik International Airport and in Reykjavik. It gives you the freedom to explore the island at your own pace and venture to places that are not accessible by public transportation. Make sure to rent a 4x4 vehicle if you plan on exploring the highlands and off-road areas.

Public Transportation: Iceland has a public bus system, called Strætó, that operates throughout the country, including Reykjavik, the Westfjords, and Akureyri. However, it can be limited in some areas and may not run frequently or at all during weekends and holidays. Bus schedules and routes are available online or at local tourist information centers.

Tours: If you prefer to sit back and let someone else do the driving, there are plenty of guided tours available in Iceland. These tours range from short-day trips to longer multi-day excursions and cover many of the popular attractions in Iceland, including the Golden Circle, the Blue Lagoon, and glacier hikes.

Taxis: Taxis are available in Reykjavik and other larger cities, but they can be expensive. However, if you are in a group, it might be more affordable than other transportation options.

Bicycles: If you are looking for a more eco-friendly and active way to explore Iceland, consider renting a bicycle. Many bike rental shops are available in Reykjavik, and some even offer guided tours.

What to Pack

Packing for a trip to Iceland can be challenging due to the country's ever-changing weather conditions. It requires careful consideration of the weather conditions and the activities you'll be participating in. I consider these materials important for a successful trip to Iceland:

Clothing

The key to packing for Iceland is to dress in layers. You'll need warm clothing to protect yourself from the chilly weather, and waterproof clothing to protect yourself from the rain. Some essentials to pack include:

- Thermal base layers: Pack thermal tops and bottoms to keep yourself warm in freezing temperatures.
- Wool sweaters: Icelandic wool sweaters are famous for their warmth and durability. Pack at least one or two to stay warm and cozy.
- Waterproof jacket and pants: Iceland experiences a lot of rain, so it's essential to pack waterproof clothing to keep yourself dry.
- Insulated jacket: A good insulated jacket will keep you warm during the day.
- Hat and gloves: A warm hat and gloves are essential to keep your head and hands warm.

- Hiking boots: Iceland has rugged terrain, so make sure you pack a pair of comfortable, sturdy hiking boots to keep your feet dry and protected.

Electronics

These electronically I'm about to suggest is very necessary for your journey to Iceland:

- Camera: Iceland is a photographer's dream destination, so don't forget to pack a camera to capture the stunning landscapes.
- Power bank: It's always a good idea to carry a power bank to keep your phone charged, especially when you're out hiking.

- Adapters: Iceland uses a Type C/F electrical outlet, so make sure you pack the right adapters for your electronics.

Personal Care Items

You'll need to pack personal care items to keep yourself clean and healthy during your trip. Some essentials include:

- Sunscreen: Despite the cold weather, the sun can still cause damage to your skin. Pack a good quality sunscreen to protect your skin from the sun's harmful rays.
- Lip balm: The cold weather can be harsh on your lips, so don't forget to pack a good quality lip balm to keep them moisturized.

- Hand sanitizer: Carry a small bottle of hand sanitizer to keep your hands clean and free of germs.
- Insect repellent: During the summer months, Iceland experiences a lot of insects, especially mosquitoes. I advise you to go with insect repellent to protect yourself from bites.

Other Essentials you might need to consider packing are:

- Travel towel: A quick-drying travel towel will come in handy during your trip, especially if you're planning on going swimming or visiting the hot springs.

- Water bottle: You can drink tap water in Iceland, so pack a reusable water bottle to stay hydrated during your trip.
- Backpack: Pack a backpack to carry all your essentials when you're out exploring.
- Cash: While credit cards are widely accepted in Iceland, it's always a good idea to carry some cash with you.

Chapter 3

Top Attractions and Activities

Iceland is an ideal destination for those who enjoy outdoor activities and are looking for thrilling adventures. There are a variety of activities available that are sure to cater to everyone's preferences. One of the top tourist attractions in Iceland is the Blue Lagoon, which is a geothermal spa with blue waters rich in minerals known to have medicinal properties. The Northern Lights are another natural wonder that is worth seeing, as they attract visitors from all over the world. The display of the aurora borealis illuminating the night sky is truly unforgettable. For those who seek adventure, Iceland offers numerous activities such as hiking, walking on glaciers, and watching whales. Iceland's magnificent national parks, including Thingvellir, Skaftafell, and Vatnajökull, offer stunning landscapes, abundant wildlife, and breathtaking scenery that visitors can explore. Iceland also provides a range of unique cultural experiences, such as Icelandic cuisine that features seafood, lamb, and other local delicacies. Visitors can also enjoy traditional Icelandic music and dance performances and learn about Iceland's Viking heritage through museums and historical sites.

The Golden Circle

The Golden Circle is a well-liked travel route in Iceland that forms a loop of around 300 kilometers and passes through some of the country's most breathtaking natural sights such as waterfalls, geysers, and national parks. Here are the main things to know about this famous Icelandic destination:

There are three primary attractions on the Golden Circle: Þingvellir National Park, Geysir Geothermal Area, and Gullfoss Waterfall. Þingvellir National Park is recognized as a UNESCO World Heritage site and it's the only place worldwide where you can observe the merging point of two tectonic plates.

The Geysir Geothermal Area is where the well-known Strokkur geyser is located, which erupts frequently every 10–15 minutes, spurting water and steam up to 30 meters high.

Gullfoss Waterfall is among Iceland's most magnificent waterfalls, plunging 32 meters down into a canyon. Other notable stops along the Golden Circle include Kerid Crater Lake, Faxi Waterfall, and Hveragerði hot springs. Traveling the Golden Circle can be accomplished as a day excursion from Reykjavik, and numerous travel operators offer guided tours that last about 8 hours.

It's advisable to visit the Golden Circle during the summer months, between May and September, when the weather is more moderate and the days are longer. Nonetheless, if you're seeking to evade the crowds, consider going in the winter months, when you can see the Northern Lights and encounter the exclusive loveliness of Iceland blanketed in snow. There's no charge for entry into Þingvellir National Park, but there is a small parking fee. The other places of interest on the

Golden Circle also have minimal entrance fees. Lastly, it's crucial to honor the natural environment and adhere to the Leave No Trace principles when touring the Golden Circle. This involves sticking to marked trails, avoiding littering, and abstaining from actions that could damage the fragile ecosystem.

The Ring Road

The Ring Road, or Route 1, is the main highway system in Iceland and circles the entire country. It is 1,332 km long and takes approximately 15-20 hours to drive, depending on the road and weather conditions. The Ring Road passes through most of Iceland's towns and cities and is the best way to explore the country.

The Ring Road was built in 1974 and is open year-round. It follows the coastline of the country, and passes through a variety of landscapes, from mountains, to glaciers, to lava fields, and more. Along the way, you'll find many of Iceland's most iconic sights and attractions, including the Blue Lagoon, Thingvellir National Park, Dettifoss Waterfall, and more.

The Ring Road is well-maintained and well-marked, making it easy to follow. Many of the roads are paved, but some of the roads are gravel, so it's important to drive carefully. There are several gas stations along the way, as well as plenty of places to stop and enjoy the scenery. When driving the Ring Road, it's important to be aware of the weather. The weather in Iceland can change quickly, and it's important to be prepared for icy roads and even snow in the winter. It's also important to be aware of the speed limits and to drive carefully, as the roads can be narrow and winding.

Exploring the Ring Road is an incredible way to experience the beauty of Iceland. It's a journey of discovery, where you can explore stunning landscapes, take in awe-inspiring sights, and get a true sense of the country's culture and history. Whether you're traveling by car, campervan, or bike, the Ring Road is an unforgettable journey.

Blue Lagoon

The Blue Lagoon is one of the most striking sites in Iceland and has become an iconic symbol of the country. Its stunning turquoise waters, surrounded by black volcanic rock, are an awe-inspiring sight. The lagoon is constantly replenished with silica-rich water, which helps to maintain the milky blue color of the lagoon. The water temperature in the lagoon remains at a comfortable 37–39 degrees Celsius, making it an ideal place for swimming and relaxing.

Visitors to the Blue Lagoon can enjoy a variety of activities, such as swimming, relaxing in the lagoon's geothermal waters, and applying therapeutic silica mud masks. The lagoon also offers several spa treatments, such as massages and facials. Visitors can also enjoy the restaurant, bar, and gift shop, as well as the lagoon's natural beauty.

The Blue Lagoon is a must-see destination for anyone visiting Iceland. It is a unique and unforgettable experience that will leave you feeling relaxed and rejuvenated. Whether you're looking for a relaxing day of soaking in the lagoon's warm waters or an invigorating spa treatment, the Blue Lagoon is an unforgettable experience.

Vatnajökull Glacier

Vatnajökull Glacier in Iceland is a must-see destination for any traveler. Located in the southeast of Iceland, the glacier is the largest in Europe and covers an area of over 8,100 km². It is part of the Vatnajökull National Park, which also encompasses the surrounding mountains, lakes, rivers, and other geological features.

Vatnajökull Glacier is an incredible sight, with its majestic ice caps and vast expanse of glacial ice stretching off into the horizon. Its beauty is breathtaking and its sheer size is awe-inspiring. The glacier is home to many of Iceland's most famous features, such as the tremendous Jökulsárlón glacial lagoon, the Skaftafell ice cave, and the largest glacier in the country, Öræfajökull. It also supports a wide range of wildlife, including reindeer, Arctic foxes, and even whales. Visitors to Vatnajökull Glacier can take part in a range of activities, from snowmobiling and hiking to camping and ice climbing. The glacier is also a great place to take in the breathtaking views of the surrounding mountains and the majestic Northern Lights, which are best seen in winter. There are also plenty of opportunities for photography, as the glacier provides an incredible backdrop to the Icelandic landscape.

Vatnajökull Glacier is an incredible natural wonder that should not be missed. Whether you're looking for adventure or just want to take in the beauty of the glacier, it's a must-see destination for any traveler.

Northern Lights

If you're looking to experience the breathtaking Northern Lights in Iceland, you're in for a treat. The Northern Lights, also known as the aurora borealis, are one of the most spectacular natural phenomena in the world and can be seen in Iceland for up to eight months of the year.

The Northern Lights are created when solar particles enter the Earth's atmosphere and interact with oxygen and nitrogen particles. As these particles move around, they create a luminescent light show in the night sky. The colors of the Northern Lights vary from bright greens, pinks, and blues, to deep purples and reds. The movement of the lights is also mesmerizing as they swirl and dance across the sky.

The best time to see the Northern Lights in Iceland is during the winter months from September to April. However, the best chance of seeing them is in the darkest months of December and January. The Northern Lights can be seen all over Iceland, but the best spots are usually away from the city lights and light pollution. Popular viewing spots include the Reykjanes Peninsula, Thingvellir National Park, and the Snaefellsnes Peninsula. It's important to remember that the Northern Lights are a natural phenomenon, so no one can guarantee that they will be visible on any given night.

To maximize your chances of seeing the Northern Lights, it's best to stay away from brightly lit areas and to keep an eye on the forecast. You can find up-to-date Aurora forecasts on the Icelandic Met Office website. It's also important to dress warmly as the Icelandic winter can be very cold.

Seeing the Northern Lights in Iceland is a once-in-a-lifetime experience and one that you will never forget. With a bit of luck and some patience, you can witness one of the most beautiful and awe-inspiring natural wonders of the world.

Whale Watching

Visiting Iceland is an incredible experience, and whale watching is one of the many activities that you can enjoy while in the country. Whale watching in Iceland is an unforgettable experience and a great way to connect with nature.

The best time to go whale watching in Iceland is from May to September when the whales come to the Icelandic waters to feed. During the summer months, the whales are most active and you are likely to see many of them. There are a few different species of whales that you can see in Iceland, including minke whales, humpback whales, and even orcas. Several different companies offer whale-watching tours in Iceland. The tours typically last around three hours and you will be taken out to sea on a boat to observe the whales. On the tour, you will be able to learn about the different species of whales, their habits, and more. The guides are knowledgeable and will be able to answer all of your questions.

When you go whale watching in Iceland, it is important to dress appropriately for the weather, as the temperatures can be quite cold. You should also bring a camera to capture some great photos of the whales.

Whale watching in Iceland is a great way to connect with nature and observe the beauty of the ocean and its wildlife. It is an experience that you will never forget and one that you will want to share with your friends and family.

Hiking and Trekking

Hiking in Iceland is a popular pastime and is a great way to get off the beaten path and explore the country. There are plenty of trails for all levels of ability, from easy day hikes to more challenging multi-day treks. Trails range from the easy and short to the more challenging, but all provide stunning views and plenty of opportunities for wildlife spotting. Be sure to check the conditions of the trail before beginning, as some can be quite slippery or muddy.

Trekking in Iceland is a great way to explore the country and experience the unique landscapes. There are many multi-day treks available, with some that last up to two weeks. These treks can be challenging, but they are also incredibly rewarding, providing the opportunity to really get to know the country and its landscapes.

No matter what type of hike or trek you choose, be sure to bring the necessary supplies and equipment. This includes plenty of water, food, a map, and appropriate clothing. Hiking and trekking in Iceland can be quite weather dependent, so make sure to check the forecast before you set out. It is also important to be aware of the terrain, as some areas can be quite difficult to navigate.

Overall, hiking and trekking in Iceland are fantastic ways to explore the country and take in its spectacular landscapes. With so many trails and multi-day treks to choose from, there is something for everyone. Just make sure you plan ahead, bring the necessary supplies, and be aware of the terrain.

With the right preparation, you're sure to have an amazing experience.

Icelandic Cuisine and Drinks

Icelandic cuisine is a unique blend of old-world traditions and modern innovation. With its unique location in the North Atlantic, Iceland has been able to create a unique culinary experience for travelers. From fresh seafood to hearty stews and traditional dishes, Iceland has something for everyone.

Seafood is a major part of Icelandic cuisine and is a must-try for travelers. Popular seafood dishes include smoked salmon, cod, haddock, and herring. Lobster, crab, and shrimp are also widely available. Icelandic lamb is another popular dish and can be found in traditional stews or as a main course. In addition to its seafood and meat dishes, Icelandic cuisine also features a variety of soups, stews, and other comfort foods. Popular soups include fish soup, lamb soup, and vegetable soup. Traditional stews include kjötsúpa, a stew made with lamb, potatoes, and vegetables, as well as plokkfiskur, a fish and potato stew.

Chapter 4

Regions and Cities

Iceland is divided into six regions, each with its distinct characteristics and attractions. From the stunning Westfjords and the rugged Highlands to the capital city of Reykjavík, there is something to entice every type of visitor to the Land of Fire and Ice.

The Westfjords region is a stunning area of dramatic fjords and soaring mountains. This landscape is home to some of the most stunning views in Iceland, including the iconic Látrabjarg cliffs – the westernmost point in Europe. The Westfjords are home to quaint fishing villages, such as Ísafjörður, and some of the country's best hiking trails. The North region of Iceland, sometimes referred to as the Diamond Circle, is a beautiful area of lush valleys and snow-capped mountains. The area is known for its natural beauty, with the majestic Lake Mývatn and the awe-inspiring Goðafoss waterfall among the highlights. The region is also home to some of Iceland's most important historical sites, such as the ancient fortifications at Hvítserkur.

The East region of Iceland is a beautiful area of rugged coastlines and volcanic mountains. The coastline of the east is home to some of the country's most breathtaking scenery, including the spectacular Jökulsárlón glacial lagoon and the incredible Fjallsárlón glacier. The East is also home to some fascinating historical sites, such as the legendary Viking settlement of Þingvellir. The

South region of Iceland is the most populous area of the country. This region is home to the capital city of Reykjavík, as well as some of the country's most beautiful landscapes, including the stunning Sólheimajökull glacier and the stunning Skógafoss waterfall. The South is also home to some of Iceland's best beaches, such as the black sand beaches of the Reynisfjara shore. The Highlands of Iceland is a unique and fascinating area of the country, with vast ranges of mountains, volcanoes, glaciers, and geysers. The Highlands are home to some of Iceland's most stunning landscapes, including the iconic Landmannalaugar hot springs and the majestic Gullfoss waterfall. The Highlands are also home to some of the country's most important historical sites, such as the ancient Viking settlement of Þjórsárdalur. The capital city of Reykjavík is the largest and most populous city in Iceland. This vibrant and cosmopolitan city is home to a wide range of attractions, from the iconic Hallgrímskirkja church to the bustling bars and restaurants of the city's famous Laugavegur street. Reykjavík is also home to some of the country's best museums and galleries, such as the National Gallery of Iceland and the Icelandic Phallological Museum. No matter what kind of experience you're looking for, there's something for everyone in Iceland's diverse regions and cities. From the majestic Westfjords to the vibrant capital of Reykjavík, there is something to captivate, inspire and intrigue every type of visitor.

Reykjavik and Surroundings

Reykjavik, Iceland's capital and largest city, is known for its stunning natural beauty and vibrant cultural activities. Located on the southwestern coast of Iceland, Reykjavik is the world's northernmost capital and is home to over two-thirds of the country's population. The city's picturesquely-situated harbor, its various museums, galleries, and nightlife, and its proximity to some of the world's most beautiful natural wonders make it a popular destination for travelers. Reykjavik is a great starting point for exploring Iceland's rugged coastline and stunning natural wonders. Just outside the city lies the Blue Lagoon, a geothermal spa that is one of the most popular attractions in the country. The lagoon's mineral-rich waters are known for their healing and therapeutic properties, and the area also features a restaurant, bar, and spa treatments. Nearby, the lava fields of Reykjanes offer a unique opportunity to explore Iceland's volcanic history, and the nearby Krýsuvík Geothermal Area is home to a variety of hot springs and mud pots.

No visit to Reykjavik is complete without exploring the golden circle, a popular tourist route that encompasses some of Iceland's most iconic natural attractions. This route includes Thingvellir National Park, where visitors can explore the rift between the North American and Eurasian tectonic plates and take in the stunning views of the area's glaciers and waterfalls. Also on the golden circle is the geyser Strokkur, which erupts every 8-10 minutes, and Gullfoss, a dramatic double-cascading waterfall.

For those looking for a more urban experience, Reykjavik offers a variety of cultural attractions. The city's art scene is particularly vibrant, with numerous galleries and museums that showcase the works of Icelandic and international artists. There is also an abundance of live music in Reykjavik, with venues ranging from small jazz bars to large music festivals. The city's nightlife is also legendary, with a range of pubs, clubs, and bars offering everything from traditional Icelandic music to international DJs.

Whether you're looking for natural beauty or urban exploration, Reykjavik and its surroundings offer something for everyone. From geothermal wonders to cultural attractions, Reykjavik and its surrounding areas provide a wide range of experiences.

South Iceland

South Iceland is an ideal destination for the adventurous traveler. The region is known for its incredible landscapes, from Icelandic glaciers to majestic waterfalls and vibrant green valleys. Natural attractions include the Golden Circle, a popular sightseeing route featuring the Strokkur Geyser, Gullfoss Waterfall, and Thingvellir National Park. Along the coast, explore the black sand beaches of Vik or take a boat trip to the volcanic island of Vestmannaeyjar. The region also boasts several charming towns and villages, including Reykjavik, Hella, and Hofn, as well as an array of outdoor activities such as hiking, skiing, and whale watching.

West Iceland

West Iceland is a breathtakingly beautiful region of Iceland, home to diverse landscapes and attractions. From the majestic Snæfellsnes Peninsula and the charming fishing villages of the Westfjords to the rugged beauty of the Vatnajökull glacier, there's something for everyone. The region is home to several national parks, natural hot springs, and a variety of exciting activities, including whale-watching, glacier hiking, and horseback riding. West Iceland is also a great place to sample the local cuisine and experience the traditional Icelandic way of life.

North Iceland

The North of Iceland is an incredibly diverse region, offering something for everyone. From the majestic snow-capped mountains to the stunning glacial rivers and waterfalls, the North of Iceland provides a unique and unforgettable experience.

The North of Iceland is home to some of the most stunning landscapes in the world, with the majestic snow-capped mountains providing a stunning backdrop for visitors. There are many activities to explore in the region, from hiking and skiing to kayaking and fishing. Adventurers and nature lovers alike will not be disappointed by the wealth of opportunities on offer.

The North of Iceland is also home to some fantastic cultural attractions, such as the famous Akureyri

Museum and the Husavik Whale Museum. Visitors can also explore the geothermal baths of Mývatn, one of the most stunning natural attractions in the country. The North of Iceland is a great place to stay, with a wide range of accommodation available. Visitors can choose from luxury hotels to cozy guesthouses and camping sites. Whatever your budget, you can find something to suit your needs. The North of Iceland is an incredibly diverse region, with something to offer everyone. Whether you are looking for a peaceful getaway or an adventure-filled holiday, the North of Iceland has something for you.

East Iceland

East Iceland is an area of Iceland characterized by its majestic landscapes, breathtaking views, and unique culture. Situated on the east coast of the island, East Iceland is home to some of the most dramatic natural scenery in the country. Whether you're looking for a relaxing beach vacation or a thrilling adventure, East Iceland has something for everyone.

The main attraction in East Iceland is its coastline, which is made up of towering sea cliffs, secluded coves, and tranquil bays. This area is known for its abundance of wildlife, including puffins, seals, and whales, which can be seen from the many lookouts along the coast. The nearby Vatnajökull Glacier is also an impressive sight, and the region is home to some of the best hiking trails in the country.

In addition to its natural beauty, East Iceland is known for its culture and history. The fishing village of Djúpivogur is one of the oldest settlements in Iceland and is home to the country's oldest church. The nearby town of Seyðisfjörður is home to a thriving arts scene and is a popular destination for music festivals. Both towns have also become popular tourist destinations, with activities ranging from whale watching to kayaking.

East Iceland is an ideal destination for travelers looking for a unique and unforgettable experience. Whether you're looking for outdoor adventure, relaxation, or cultural exploration, East Iceland has something for everyone

Chapter 5

Practical Tips for Traveling in Iceland

Money and Currency

Iceland uses the Icelandic króna as its official currency, abbreviated as ISK. The króna is divided into 100 aurar. The value of the króna is closely tied to the Euro and fluctuates with the exchange rate. ATMs and currency exchange kiosks are available in large cities and tourist areas, and almost all businesses accept major credit and debit cards. Major currencies such as the US dollar, Euro, and British pound are easy to exchange, but other currencies may be difficult to exchange and incur higher fees. It is important to note that Iceland is an expensive country to visit. The cost of food, lodging, and entertainment are all higher than in other parts of Europe. It is best to plan and budget accordingly for a trip to Iceland.

It is also important to note that tipping is not customary in Iceland. In most restaurants, a service charge is included in the bill, and tipping is not expected. However, if you feel your service was especially good, you may leave a small gratuity. Overall, Iceland is a great destination to visit, but it is important to be aware of the cost of living and the currency exchange rate before you go. With some careful planning and budgeting, you can have an amazing time in Iceland!

Language

Icelandic is the official language of Iceland, spoken by the majority of its population. It is a North

Germanic language, closely related to Faroese and West Norse dialects. It is closest living relative is Faroese, and both are descended from Old Norse. Icelandic is the national language and one of the two official languages of Iceland, along with English.

Icelandic has been spoken in Iceland since the settlement of the island in the 9th century and is still the language of everyday life in the country. It is a very conservative language, with many of its words and structures closely related to those of Old Norse. Icelanders are very proud of their language and its distinctiveness, and it is an important part of the national identity.

Most Icelanders can speak both English and Icelandic. English is widely spoken and understood, especially among younger people. English is also used in the business world, with much of the business literature being in English.

The written language is regulated by the Icelandic Language Institute, which publishes spelling and grammar guides. The language is also regulated by the Icelandic Language Council, which is responsible for making recommendations to the government about language policies.

Icelandic is written in the Latin alphabet, with three additional letters – ð, þ, and æ. Several diacritics are used to indicate short vowels and long vowels.

Icelandic is a very phonetic language, with words pronounced exactly as they're written. This makes it relatively easy for foreigners to learn to pronounce Icelandic words.

Safety and Emergencies

Iceland is a safe and peaceful country with a low crime rate. The emergency services are well-trained and equipped to deal with any situation.

The country has an emergency number which is 112 and this number is for police, fire, and ambulance services. Emergency services are available 24/7 and can be reached by calling the 112 number. It's important to note that the police in Iceland are unarmed. The police in Iceland focus on solving criminal cases, not preventing them.

The weather in Iceland can be unpredictable, and it's important to be prepared when traveling in the country. Make sure to check the weather forecast before traveling and be prepared for any sudden changes. In the event of a natural disaster, such as an earthquake, tsunami, or volcanic eruption, the Ministry of Foreign Affairs provides updated information on its website.

Finally, if you have any medical emergencies while traveling in Iceland, the national health service is available 24/7. The service includes several hospitals, health centers, and emergency centers.

Etiquette and Customs

1. Greeting: When greeting someone, a handshake and a polite "hello" is the norm.

2. Table manners: Table manners are quite relaxed. It is better to wait for the host to start eating first.

3. Gifts: It is appropriate to give a small gift when invited to someone's home. Examples of these are flowers, chocolates, and wine.

4. Public behavior: Public behavior should always be respectful and polite. Romantic shows of love outside are generally considered inappropriate.

5. Language: English is widely spoken in Iceland, but it is polite to learn a few basic phrases in the local language.

6. Alcohol: Alcohol is widely available, but drinking in public is generally not tolerated.

7. Tipping: Tipping is not expected in Iceland, but it is appreciated.

8. Clothing: Clothing should be modest and appropriate for the season. Shorts and tank tops are not generally worn in public.

9. Nature: Iceland's natural beauty should be respected. It is illegal to remove rocks, plants, or anything else from the natural environment.

Health and Medical Services

Iceland offers a comprehensive range of health and medical services to travelers and residents alike. The country has a modern health care system that is provided by the Icelandic Health Care System. The system provides both primary and specialist care. Everyone who is a citizen or a permanent resident is eligible to receive free healthcare.

The primary care services are provided by general practitioners and specialists, who will refer you to a hospital if necessary. All major hospitals in Iceland are equipped with the latest technology and are staffed by highly trained and experienced professionals. Emergency services are accessible 24/7. In the event of an emergency, the local emergency number is 112. Iceland also offers a range of specialized medical services including mental health care, dentistry, and optometry. There are also several specialized clinics for specific medical conditions.

It is important to note that there is no public health insurance in Iceland. All medical services must be paid for out-of-pocket and you should plan for any unexpected medical costs. If you have travel insurance, check to see if it covers medical expenses in Iceland.

Finally, it is important to note that Iceland has strict laws governing the sale and possession of medications. If you are carrying any prescription drugs, make sure you have a valid prescription from a doctor in your own country.

Chapter 6

Conclusion and Final Recommendations

Top Do's and Don'ts

Do's

1. Follow good hiking etiquette and stay on marked paths when exploring Iceland's natural beauty.

2. Make sure to dress for the weather. Iceland can be unpredictable; pack layers and waterproof clothing.

3. Respect the local wildlife and don't try to feed or touch any animals you come across.

4. Purchase a SIM card to have access to the internet and make sure to download offline maps for navigation.

5. Take advantage of the country's incredible food and try the local delicacies such as skyr and hákarl.

6. Don't forget to bring a refillable water bottle and a power adapter for Iceland's power outlets.

7. Make sure to purchase travel insurance to cover any unexpected accidents or losses.

Don'ts

1. Don't forget to bring a passport if you're planning to cross any international borders.

2. Don't litter or leave any trace of your presence in Iceland's fragile nature.

3. Don't forget to take the necessary safety precautions when exploring Iceland's glaciers and ice caves.

4. Don't forget to charge your phone or camera battery before you leave for the day.

5. Don't forget to be aware of the local laws and customs while in Iceland.

6. Don't forget to check the weather forecast before embarking on any outdoor activities.

7. Don't forget to apply for a visa if you're planning to stay in Iceland for longer than three months.

Off-The-Beaten-Path Destinations

Landmannalaugar: Located in the Fjallabak Nature Reserve, this area is home to hot springs, lava fields, and colorful mountains.

2. Westfjords: This remote part of Iceland offers spectacular views of the Arctic Ocean.

3. Hornstrandir Nature Reserve: Located in the far north of Iceland, this area is known for its rugged beauty and abundant wildlife.

4. Ásbyrgi Canyon: This horseshoe-shaped canyon is home to a variety of flora and fauna, and is a great spot for hiking.

5. Snæfellsjökull National Park: This park offers stunning views of the Snæfellsjökull Glacier, as well as a variety of geological formations.

6. Látrabjarg Cliffs: These cliffs offer some of the best birdwatching in the world, as well as stunning views of the sea.

7. Mývatn: This area is known for its unique landscape, which includes geothermal vents, lava fields, and volcanic craters.

8. Þingvellir National Park: This UNESCO World Heritage Site is home to the oldest parliament in the world, as well as a variety of unique geological features.

9. Jökulsárlón Glacier Lagoon: This lagoon is home to a variety of icebergs and is a great spot for kayaking or boat tours.

Sustainable Tourism Practices

1. Respect local cultures and customs: Be respectful of the locals and their culture, customs, and traditions.

2. Give back to the local economy: Consider choosing locally-owned accommodations and restaurants, and patronizing local businesses.

3. Minimize your carbon footprint: Try to minimize your impact on the environment by using public transportation, carpooling, or taking part in a carbon offset program.

4. Reduce your water use: Use water-saving methods in your accommodations and limit your water use whenever possible.

5. Respect nature: Make sure to stay on designated trails, properly dispose of all waste, and don't remove any plants or wildlife.

6. Respect wildlife: Do not disturb or approach any wildlife, and make sure to stay a safe distance away.

7. Leave no trace: Make sure to leave the area as you found it, and don't leave any litter behind.

8. Get involved: Support local initiatives and organizations that aim to protect and preserve the environment.

Conclusion

Iceland is a land of extremes, and it's no surprise that it is one of the most popular tourist destinations in the world. With an incredible landscape, diverse wildlife, and unique culture, it has something for everyone. Whether you're looking for adventure, relaxation, or something in between, Iceland is the perfect destination for your next getaway. From the awe-inspiring glaciers of the south to the rugged beauty of the north, Iceland is sure to be an unforgettable experience. So, what are you waiting for? Start planning your trip to Iceland today and explore a land like no other!

Printed in Great Britain
by Amazon